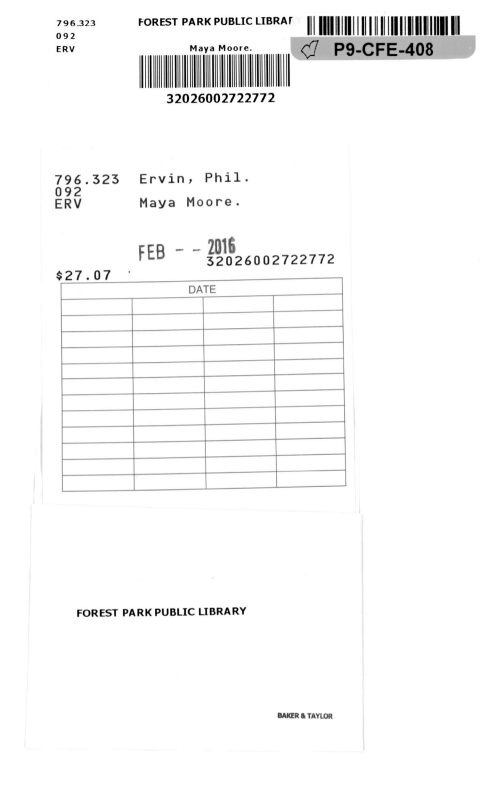

DATE			

MAYA MOORE

BY PHIL ERVIN

SportsZone
An Imprint of Abdo Publishing
abdopublishing.com

abdopublishing.com

Published by Abdo Publishing, a division of ABDO, PO Box 398166, Minneapolis, Minnesota 55439. Copyright © 2016 by Abdo Consulting Group, Inc. International copyrights reserved in all countries. No part of this book may be reproduced in any form without written permission from the publisher. SportsZone™ is a trademark and logo of Abdo Publishing.

Printed in the United States of America, North Mankato, Minnesota
032015
092015

Cover Photo: Jessica Hill/AP Images
Interior Images: Jessica Hill/AP Images, 1, 10, 17, 18; Jason Getz/Atlanta Journal-Constitution/AP Images, 4; Stacy Bengs/AP Images, 7; Joey Ivansco/Atlanta Journal-Constitution/AP Images, 9; Phil Hawkins/Cal Sport Media/AP Images, 13; Chris Morrison/AP Images, 14; Eric Gay/AP Images, 21; China Topix/AP Images, 23; John Froschauer/AP Images, 24; Renee Jones Schneider/The Star Tribune/AP Images, 27; Anthony Nesmith/Cal Sport Media/AP Images, 29

Editor: Nick Rebman
Series Designer: Craig Hinton

Library of Congress Control Number: 2015931751

Cataloging-in-Publication Data
Ervin, Phil.
 Maya Moore: WNBA champion / Phil Ervin.
   p. cm. -- (Playmakers)
Includes bibliographical references and index.
ISBN 978-1-62403-840-2
1. Moore, Maya--Juvenile literature. 2. Basketball players--United States--Biography--Juvenile literature. 3. Women's National Basketball Association--Juvenile literature.   I. Title.
796.323092--dc23
[B]   2015931751

TABLE OF CONTENTS

CHAPTER 1

FROM THE MIDWEST TO THE SOUTH

Maya Moore looked ready to play. A white headband held back her hair. Long sleeves covered her arms. Her Jordan shoes were laced up tight.

Maya's team, the Minnesota Lynx, had a big game that night. It was the Women's National Basketball Association (WNBA) playoffs. But before the game started, a ceremony took place. Maya was getting an award. She had been named the

A 16-year-old Maya Moore makes a layup for Collins Hill High School.

2014 WNBA Most Valuable Player (MVP). She thanked her mother. She thanked her teammates. Maya was nervous through the entire ceremony. She could not wait for the game to start.

Finally, it was time to play. And Maya did what she does best. She scored 26 points. The Lynx beat the San Antonio Stars 88–84.

Maya was a very energetic child. But she and her mother lived in a small apartment. Sometimes her mother had a hard time stopping Maya from running around inside. So her mother put a small basketball hoop on the front door. After that, basketball was Maya's favorite sport.

Maya had worked hard to become the best player in women's basketball. But her journey started 25 years earlier. Maya was born on June 11, 1989. She lived in Jefferson City, Missouri. She did not have any brothers or sisters. It was just Maya and her mother at home.

Moore holds up her MVP award before a WNBA playoff game in 2014.

But they were not alone. Maya had lots of younger cousins. She used to babysit them. When something went wrong, Maya usually took the blame. Babysitting taught her responsibility at a young age. It also taught her the value of leadership.

Maya first picked up a basketball when she was three years old. She joined her first team when she was seven. Maya spent four seasons with this team. She was one of the tallest players. This helped her score more points than any of her teammates.

Maya often dreamed of playing in the WNBA. The league started in 1997 when she was eight. An uncle gave Maya a

WNBA game ball. She brought it with her to almost every tournament she played in.

> *"I think I really do learn more from her than I have taught her about leadership."* —Kathryn Moore, Maya's mother

Maya worked hard to develop her skills. She practiced her jump shot. She practiced dribbling and passing. She practiced her defensive skills, too.

A big change happened when Maya was in sixth grade. She and her mother moved to North Carolina. They lived there for a year. After that, they moved to Georgia. This was where Maya really became a basketball star.

In 2005, she started playing for the Georgia Metros. With Maya's help, the Metros won several national tournaments. In one game, Maya scored 42 points.

Maya's popularity began spreading. Experts thought she could be a big star. So did college coaches.

Maya started for the Lady Eagles all four years of high school.

Maya went to Collins Hill High School. Her team won three state championships. During Maya's four years there, her team won 125 games. It lost only three. Maya was one of the top college recruits in the country.

Maya worked hard in the classroom, too. She graduated with a perfect 4.0 grade-point average. That means she got As in all of her classes.

Lots of college coaches wanted Maya on their teams. Many schools offered her scholarships. Maya chose the University of Connecticut. It ended up being a very good decision.

Maya Moore

CHAPTER 2

HELPING MOLD A DYNASTY

Some basketball players are good shooters. Others dribble well. Others are good passers. Some are best at defense. Maya Moore did everything. She could play almost every position. This helped the Connecticut Huskies win a lot of games.

Moore had a great season during her first year of college. Some say it was the best freshman season in women's college basketball history. She averaged

Moore dunks the ball during her junior year at Connecticut.

17.8 points per game. She made lots of three-pointers. With Moore's help, the Huskies reached the Final Four.

In Moore's second season, the Huskies went undefeated. They also won the national championship. Moore was named the national Player of the Year.

The next season went the same way. Again, the Huskies did not lose a game. Moore was a tough competitor. But she was also a good person off the court. She earned good grades. She got several academic awards.

During Moore's last season, Connecticut won its ninetieth straight game. That set a National Collegiate Athletic Association (NCAA) record. But the Huskies lost in the Final Four. Still, Moore had a great year. She scored the most points of her college career. She also won her second Player of the Year Award.

> "She's just one of those great athletes who is able to block everything out except what's important. 'My team needs me to do this tonight.' And she sets her mind to it and she does it." —Huskies coach Geno Auriemma

Moore dribbles the ball in a game against Stanford in 2010.

On her own, Moore showed speed, strength, and ability. She had a lot of help, though. Her coach was Geno Auriemma. He is one of the greatest basketball coaches ever. Moore also played with talented teammates. Several of them went on to play in the WNBA.

Moore was now done with college. She was ready to become a professional basketball player. Every WNBA team wanted her. And one team really needed her.

Maya Moore

CHAPTER 3

RISE TO GREATNESS

The Minnesota Lynx were struggling in 2010. The team missed the WNBA playoffs for a sixth straight year. It was clear the Lynx needed a star player. They found one in Maya Moore.

Minnesota had the first pick in the 2011 WNBA Draft. There is usually some mystery about who the first pick will be. But this time was different. Everyone knew Minnesota would choose Moore. She was clearly the best player.

Moore drives hard to the basket during her rookie season with the Minnesota Lynx.

By this time, Moore was already very popular. She signed a shoe contract with Nike's Jordan Brand. She was the first woman to do that.

Moore hoped to do in Minnesota what she did in Connecticut: win championships. But she had to adjust to professional basketball. WNBA players are bigger, stronger, and faster than college players. Moore had the help of her coach, Cheryl Reeve. She also learned from her teammates, including star veterans Lindsay Whalen and Seimone Augustus. They taught Moore all about playing in the WNBA.

It did not take Moore long to make a mark. She started all 34 of Minnesota's games as a rookie.

Moore's best friend on the team was Taj McWilliams-Franklin. McWilliams-Franklin was a team leader. She taught the other players how take care of their bodies. Her teammates

Moore was the WNBA's Rookie of the Month in both July and August 2011. She played in the 2011 WNBA All-Star Game, too.

Maya Moore, *center*, sits with Auriemma, *left*, and her mother, *right*, during the 2011 WNBA Draft.

called her "Mama Taj." She was 40 years old. Moore was only 22. McWilliams-Franklin often told Moore she was a special player. Moore proved her right. She had a fantastic season. She won the WNBA Rookie of the Year Award.

Moore helped the Lynx win 27 games. They had the WNBA's best record. This gave them home-court advantage in the playoffs. First they beat the San Antonio Stars. Then they beat the Phoenix Mercury. Now it was time for the WNBA Finals.

The Lynx had never played for a championship. But Maya Moore had.

Maya Moore

CHAPTER 4

MORE CHAMPIONSHIPS

The 2011 WNBA Finals had arrived. The Minnesota Lynx played the Atlanta Dream. The first team to win three games would be the champion. These games were the biggest of Maya Moore's life. But she was not intimidated. She had learned all about playing in big games at Connecticut.

The Lynx won the first two games in the series. They went to Atlanta with the chance for a sweep. Moore had spent part of her childhood in Atlanta.

Moore makes a shot during a 2013 game against the Connecticut Sun.

So she had lots of family and friends there. They came to watch her play. Moore did not disappoint. She scored 15 points. That included a key three-pointer in the fourth quarter. Minnesota won the game 73–67.

The Lynx were champions for the first time. After the team flew back to Minnesota, a parade was held in their honor. It would not be the last one.

Moore's parents were athletes, too. Her mother played volleyball in college. Her father was a basketball player at Rutgers University.

Moore played in Spain after her first WNBA season. Many WNBA players play overseas during the winter. This helps them earn extra money. Moore did very well in Spain. Her team won the EuroLeague title.

Fans were drawn to Moore's skills. They also liked her personality. People started saying she could be the best women's basketball player ever.

Moore, *front*, poses with her teammates after winning the gold medal in the 2012 Olympics in London, England.

Moore uses that popularity to do good. She believes it is important to give back to the community. So she supports many charities. She works with Athletes in Action. This group blends sports and faith. She also takes part in WNBA Cares programs. Every year she holds a basketball camp. The camp is called the

> *"It's not necessarily about outworking the person standing across from me. It's outworking that voice inside of my mind that says, 'I'm too tired. I don't feel like doing this. I can settle.'"* —Maya Moore

Maya Moore Academy. She works with United Way, too. She talks about the importance of reading.

The WNBA took a break halfway through the 2012 season. It was time for the Olympic Games in London, England. Moore was an important part of Team USA. She was playing in the Olympics for the first time.

There were some familiar faces on the team. Two Lynx teammates were on the roster. And the team was coached by Geno Auriemma. Moore did very well in the Olympics. She helped Team USA win the gold medal.

The WNBA season continued after the Olympics. Minnesota made it back to the WNBA Finals that year. But this time, the Lynx lost to the Indiana Fever.

After the season, Moore went overseas again. She joined a team in China. That team also won a championship. Maya was

Moore gives high fives to fans at a basketball game in China.

easily the best player in the league. She averaged 45 points per game. In one game she scored 60 points.

Moore had become a world-class athlete. But she did not let it change who she was.

Maya Moore

CHAPTER 5

STAYING HUMBLE

Lots of young girls wait for Maya Moore after home games. They form a long line. They want to see their favorite player. Moore is usually tired. But she always stops to say hello. She signs autographs. Sometimes she takes pictures. She is a fan favorite in Minnesota and around the world.

The attention has not changed her, though. Moore believes it is important to stay humble. And she continues to work hard. She credits her

In 2014, Moore led the WNBA with an average of 23.9 points per game.

teammates and coaches. She continues to practice her faith. And she knows she can accomplish even more.

That mindset helped her greatly in 2013. Her numbers improved again. She averaged 18.5 points per game. This made her one of the best scorers in the WNBA.

Since 2011, Moore's No. 23 jersey has been one of the WNBA's best-selling.

Moore took two big steps in her career. She became a better defender. This helped her guard more players than she had before. She also made better decisions on the court. A more nutritious diet helped her, too. Moore often talks about how to eat well when she speaks at events.

Lindsay Whalen was still on the team in 2013. So was Seimone Augustus. And Cheryl Reeve was still the coach. Together, the Lynx had the league's best record. They did it for

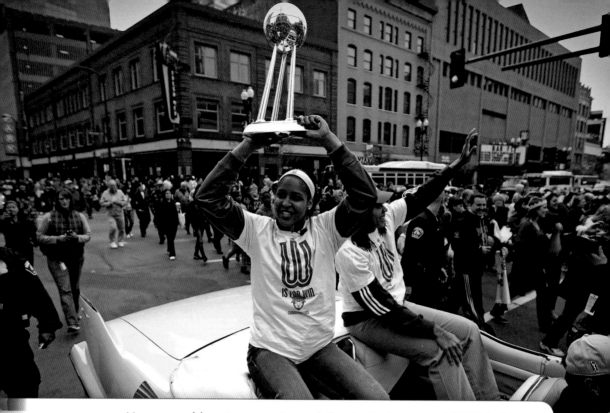

Moore and her teammates celebrate their second WNBA title during a parade in Minnesota.

the third year in a row. Minnesota did not lose a single game in the playoffs. They swept Atlanta in the WNBA Finals again. They won their second title in three years.

Moore was named the WNBA Finals MVP. She scored 20.9 points per game during the playoffs. As usual, she saved her best for the biggest moments. The Lynx were champions again. Moore and her teammates got to ride in another parade.

Moore then went back to China. She played her second season there. Her team won the league title once again. It seemed like Moore could not lose!

The 2014 season was Moore's fourth in the WNBA. She led the league in scoring. She played in her third All-Star Game. In one game, she scored a team-record 48 points.

It was not hard for reporters to choose the league MVP. They voted for Moore. She accepted the award before the 2014 playoffs.

"As athletes, we have a platform. We have an influence on younger kids, whether they're athletes or not. Sometimes people need a little extra attention and opportunity to get where they want to be. To be able to do that for someone else feels really good." —Maya Moore on giving back to the community

As a team, Minnesota came up short this time. The Phoenix Mercury beat the Lynx in the playoffs. The Mercury then won the WNBA championship. Moore missed the finals for the first time. So she felt very motivated to help Minnesota get back.

Moore has made many great plays as a member of Team USA.

Later that year, Moore was back with Team USA. And she helped the team win another gold medal. It was at the FIBA World Championship. Moore scored 18 points in the gold medal game. She also earned MVP honors. Reeve helped coach the team. Whalen and Augustus played alongside Moore.

Moore's goals are simple. She wants to keep getting better. And she wants to win more championships. She is already one of the best women's basketball players ever. But even the best can improve.

FUN FACTS AND QUOTES

- Moore finished her college career with all kinds of honors. She was a two-time national player of the year. She became the second player in NCAA history to be named an All-American four times. And she won more games than any other women's college basketball player.

- As of 2014, Moore has played in three WNBA All-Star Games. In 2014, she received more fan votes than any other player.

- *"I love living in the moment, and after the season's over, there will be a time to reflect and enjoy things. But I want to make sure that I don't miss anything in the present because I'm getting comfortable with what the outside is saying."* —Maya Moore during the 2013 season

- Moore likes hanging out with her teammates. They have a lot of fun during road trips. One of her college teammates, Caroline Doty, said Moore's three favorite things to do were "eat, sleep, sing."

- Maya's mother, Kathryn, has Lynx season tickets. She attends most of Minnesota's home games. Sometimes, she waves a blue pom-pom. Kathryn Moore looks a lot like her daughter. She talks like her, too. Maya's mother has always been one of her biggest supporters.

WEBSITES

To learn more about Playmakers, visit **booklinks.abdopublishing.com**. These links are routinely monitored and updated to provide the most current information available.

accomplish
To complete a goal or draw praise from people.

contract
A written, signed agreement between people or groups of people.

EuroLeague
The highest professional basketball league in Europe for women's teams.

Final Four
The last four teams in the NCAA tournament, which starts with 64 teams.

intimidated
Scared or worried.

leadership
The ability to lead or guide a group.

mindset
A set of certain thoughts or ideas.

motivated
Driven to act a certain way or complete certain tasks.

NCAA
National Collegiate Athletic Association. This is the group in charge of college sports.

nutritious
Healthy for a person to eat or drink.

recruits
High school athletes whom colleges want for their teams.

scholarships
Payments for college education in exchange for athletes playing.

undefeated
Going through a certain set of games without losing.

world-class
Being one of the best in the world.

INDEX

FURTHER RESOURCES

Bird, Sue, and Greg Brown. *Sue Bird: Be Yourself*. Kirkland, WA: Positively for Kids, 2004.

Editors of Sports Illustrated Kids Magazine. *Sports Illustrated Kids Slam Dunk: The Top 10 of Everything in Basketball*. New York: Time Home Entertainment Inc., 2014.

Silverman, Drew. *Basketball*. Minneapolis: Abdo Publishing, 2012.